The Shocking
Story of
Electricity

THIS EDITION
Editorial Management by Oriel Square
Produced for DK by WonderLab Group LLC
Jennifer Emmett, Erica Green, Kate Hale, *Founders*

Editors Grace Hill Smith, Libby Romero, Maya Myers, Michaela Weglinski;
Photography Editors Kelley Miller, Annette Kiesow, Nicole DiMella; **Managing Editor** Rachel Houghton;
Designers Project Design Company; **Researcher** Michelle Harris; **Copy Editor** Lori Merritt;
Indexer Connie Binder; **Proofreader** Larry Shea; **Reading Specialist** Dr. Jennifer Albro;
Curriculum Specialist Elaine Larson

Published in the United States by DK Publishing
1745 Broadway, 20th Floor, New York, NY 10019

Copyright © 2023 Dorling Kindersley Limited
DK, a Division of Penguin Random House LLC
23 24 25 26 10 9 8 7 6 5 4 3 2 1
001-333929-Oct/2023

A catalog record for this book
is available from the Library of Congress.
HC ISBN: 978-0-7440-7317-1
PB ISBN: 978-0-7440-7328-7

DK books are available at special discounts when purchased in bulk for sales promotions, premiums,
fundraising, or educational use. For details, contact: DK Publishing Special Markets,
1745 Broadway, 20th Floor, New York, NY 10019
SpecialSales@dk.com

Printed and bound in China

The publisher would like to thank the following for their kind permission to reproduce their images:
a=above; c=center; b=below; l=left; r=right; t=top; b/g=background
123RF.com: Mykola Mazuryk 36tl, Vladimir Salman 37tr, Tomasz Wyszolmirski 40tl; **Alamy Stock Photo:** Courtesy Everett
Collection 14-15t, Science History Images 26tl, Science History Images / Photo Researchers 9bl; **Dorling Kindersley:** Ruth Jenkinson
/ RGB Research Limited 17crb, Clive Streeter / The Science Museum, London 23t, 26tr, Gary Ombler / Whipple Museum of History of
Science, Cambridge 8tl; **Dreamstime.com:** Adisa 30cl, Agaliza 25tr, 37cra, Antartis 40-41b, BrightonGranny 35, Byelikova 39cr,
• µ µє 12tl, Designua 22tl, Luisa Vallon Fumi 21tr, Evgeny Glyanenko 41tr, Ibreakstock 31bl, Krutenyuk 3b, Matthieuclouis 6clb,
Maximus117 6tl, Al-fadzly Shah Mohd Nor 17tr, Stephan Pietzko 32tl, Pressmaster 6-7b, Olivier Le Queinec 27tr, Nikita Rublev 26clb,
Sebalos 16clb, Anton Shulgin 42cr, Stnazkul 15br, Tonyv3112 34tl, Worachaiy 43tr, Yourthstock 7cla, Yuming Zhu 12-13b;
Getty Images: Archive Photos / Buyenlarge / Napoleon Sarony 29tr, Archive Photos / Stock Montage 22tr, Bettmann 27b, 30-31t, 38tl,
DEA / G. DAGLI ORTI / De Agostini 16tl, John Moore / Staff 33cr, Photo12 / Universal Images Group 19tl;
Getty Images / iStock: amriphoto 1b, E+ / joecicak 9tr, E+ / tdub_video 43br, Freder 30tl, Mlenny 38br, Artur Nichiporenko 4-5;
NASA: JPL 45tl, JPL-Caltech 45bl; **Science Photo Library:** Martyn F. Chillmaid 10tc, Mikkel Juul Jensen 24-25b, Royal Institution Of
Great Britain 22br, Sheila Terry 17bl, 20br; **Shutterstock.com:** Rod Adolfo 32r, Everett Collection 28br, 29crb, Mark Fisher 42tl,
fridas 20cla, grayjay 10tl, milatas 14cla, zizou7 28tl

Cover images: *Front:* **Shutterstock.com:** mollyw; *Back:* **Shutterstock.com:** NVRs cla

All other images © Dorling Kindersley
For more information see: www.dkimages.com

For the curious
www.dk.com

The Shocking
Story of
Electricity

Suzanne Sherman

CONTENTS

ALL CHARGED UP

Has this ever happened to you? You are happily reading or playing, and then suddenly the room goes black. You try to turn on the light, but it's still dark. You look around the other rooms, and they are dark, too. The power is out!

Power outages can be fun for a while. You can light some candles with your family or try to read by flashlight. But if you start feeling hot, you can't turn on the air conditioning. That needs electricity.

Force of Nature
For millions of years, humans encountered only natural forms of electricity, such as electric fish and lightning. To learn more about lightning and how it works, see page 12.

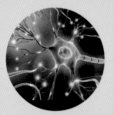

Electricity in You
You have small amounts of electricity in your body! Your brain relies on electricity to send and receive signals to and from the rest of your body.

You can play on a device until the battery runs out. But it needs electricity to recharge.

If the adults in your life work on computers, they can't do their jobs. Computers need electricity, too.

We rely on electrical power. When we don't have it, everything seems to stop. But it hasn't always been that way. Not so long ago, people didn't have the science or engineering knowledge to use electricity.

Shocking Fish
Electric eels are a type of electric fish. They have special organs that produce electrical pulses that they use to stun their prey.

The Protector
The earliest records of electric fish date all the way back to ancient Egypt. Depictions of the electric catfish of the Nile River adorn certain tombs, the oldest from 2750 BCE.

Sparks from a Jar
Dutch scientist Pieter van Musschenbroek developed the Leyden jar in 1746. At the time, he was working in his lab at the University of Leyden. That's how the invention, a predecessor to the modern battery, got its name.

Electricity was never invented. It has always existed in nature. For thousands of years, people have described its mysterious powers. They have watched lightning strike from the sky and have seen it cause fires and destruction.

Centuries ago, electricity was viewed only as a mighty force of nature, not something people could use. No one knew what electricity was, let alone how to control it.

In the 1740s, American inventor Benjamin Franklin was curious about electricity. He wanted to make it useful. A friend gave Franklin a Leyden jar, which, back then, was a glass jar of water with a cork in the top and a wire that dipped into the water.

The jar stored electricity and, when touched, it could deliver a small shock, almost like a miniature lightning bolt. Franklin was captivated by the jar and began learning everything he could about electricity.

Ben Franklin

Party Tricks
Franklin was enthralled by the acts of a showman named Archibald Spencer. Spencer traveled around the world performing "electric magic tricks." In his biggest stunt, he suspended a boy from the ceiling and rubbed his feet with a glass rod. Feathers stuck to the boy's nose and sparks flew when people tried to touch him!

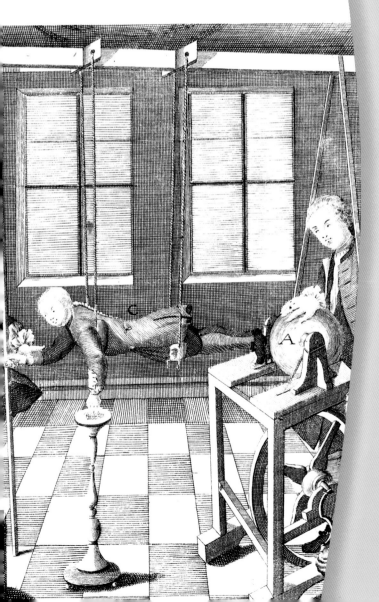

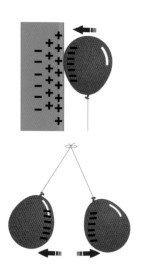

Just like Franklin's spider, a stream of water interacts with a glass rod that has an electric charge.

Pulls and Pushes
Opposite charges attract, or pull together. But two like charges push away from each other, or repel. That means that two negatively charged objects, or two positively charged objects, will push each other away.

Spidey Moves
Franklin's spider didn't just wiggle. It flew toward a wire, bent its legs around the wire, sprung off, and jumped toward another wire on the table!

The problem was that little scientific information was written about electricity yet. So, Franklin did his own experiments and busily wrote about his observations. He even devised a trick, just for fun. Franklin created a "spider" out of cork and thread. He hung the spider over a glass vial, and magically, the spider began to move around as if it were alive.

But this wasn't magic. It was science. To perform the trick, Franklin "electrified" the glass vial, possibly rubbing it with a wool cloth. Franklin didn't know it at the time, but he was using static electricity to make his spider move. Static electricity occurs when two different objects come into contact with each other. When the objects are rubbed together, static electricity can build up.

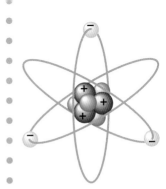

The electrical charge in static electricity comes from electrons. Electrons are extremely tiny particles with a negative charge that surround an atom's nucleus. Some materials, like glass, lose electrons easily and become positively charged. Others, like wool, pick up electrons easily and get a negative charge. Oppositely charged objects attract each other. They can make each other move.

In Franklin's trick, both the glass and the spider had a positive charge. The like charges repelled, making the spider hop about.

Like glass, human hair loses electrons easily. If you rub a balloon against your head, electrons move from your hair to the balloon, and your hair stands up!

Parts of an Atom
All matter is made of tiny particles called atoms, and atoms are composed of even tinier particles. Protons carry a positive charge (+), while electrons carry a negative charge (-). Neutrons are neutral. They have no charge. Together with protons, they form the core, or nucleus, of the atom.

Defining Electricity
Franklin was the first person to use the words "positive" and "negative" to explain electric charges.

11

BOLTS AND VOLTS

Though lightning was known to be quite dangerous, Franklin was fascinated by it. Like his electric spiders, lightning is caused by static electricity. Electrons build up high in clouds after rising water droplets bump against falling ice crystals, making the crystals positively charged. The charge becomes so unbalanced and extreme that when the electrons rebalance themselves ... BOOM!

Your Own Little Lightning
A plasma ball is a toy that works similarly to lightning. It is a clear glass ball filled with gases. It has a device in the center that builds up an electric charge. When someone touches the outside of the ball, the electrons discharge toward their finger, creating a mini lightning bolt.

A streak of light brightens the sky. Franklin noticed that lightning often discharges to pointy, metal objects. He was determined to put that observation to good use. He began attaching pointy metal rods to the tops of houses and extending them all the way into the ground. When lightning struck the rods, it traveled to the ground instead of hitting and burning down the house.

Franklin had invented the lightning rod as we know it. His invention still protects buildings around the world today.

A lightning bolt is a stream of electrons shooting toward the ground or between clouds as they spread themselves back out.

Electric Fire
Have you ever seen sparks between blankets at night? Some blanket materials lose electrons easily. When those blankets rub against another material, electrons build up and then zap back. You can see tiny flashes of light and may even hear crackling noises. In his writings, Franklin called these flashes "electric fire."

Striking Statistic
A typical bolt of lightning carries about 300 million volts of electricity.

Thunderstorm Safety
Always seek shelter when you see lightning or hear thunder. If you can't go inside, crouch with your feet on the ground far from any trees.

In 1752, Franklin conducted his most famous—and dangerous—experiment. As the story goes, he was standing near a steeple on top of a church during a thunderstorm. His son, William, was next to him. The metal steeple would act as a lightning rod, he reasoned.

The storm clouds were high in the sky. So, Franklin tied a metal key to a kite string and flew the kite. Floating dangerously close to the electrically charged clouds, the metal key attracted electrons and became charged itself.

Thunderstorm Dangers
If you're stuck outside during a thunderstorm, stay away from high places and isolated trees that will attract lightning. Avoid metal and water. Both of those materials accept electrons easily and will attract lightning, too. Concrete can be dangerous, too, because it often has metal inside of it.

CRACK! The key sent a spark straight to Franklin's knuckles. William was the only one to see it happen.

Franklin proved that lightning was a form of electricity, but he was lucky to live. If the key had been struck by a bolt of lightning, Franklin would have been killed. Millions of volts of electricity would have traveled through the key and straight through his body.

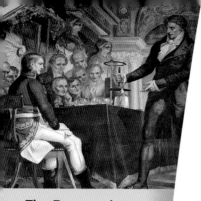

STORING ELECTRICITY

By the late 1700s, scientists knew that electricity held immense power. But they didn't know where electricity came from.

Then, in 1771, Italian scientist Luigi Galvani was conducting an experiment on a dead frog. He touched the frog's leg with two different metals—and the frog's leg moved! Galvani did not realize that he had sent a stream of electrons through the frog's leg with the metals. He concluded that the movement was caused by "animal electricity." His friend, Alessandro Volta, didn't think that was correct. So, he did experiments of his own.

Volta set out to prove that his friend was wrong. In the process, he made a huge discovery. By connecting different metals and liquids in a certain order, he created a steady stream of electrons. This is called an electric current. Volta used this knowledge to build the first electric battery, known as a voltaic pile.

It consisted of discs of alternating metals, such as copper and zinc, with a cloth soaked in salt water placed between each layer. Zinc loses electrons, copper accepts them, and salt helps electrons move. By stacking these materials, Volta caused electrons to move steadily from one end to the other.

Stay in Your Lane
An insulator is a material that does not allow electrons to move easily. Plastic is an insulator. Insulators are useful for things like coatings around wires.

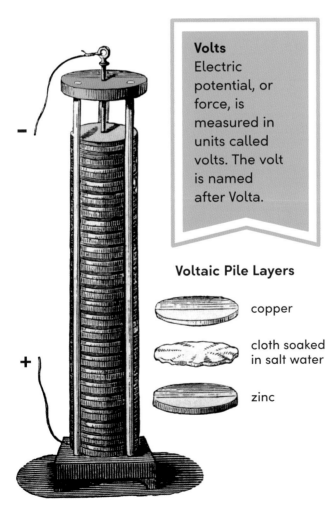

Volts
Electric potential, or force, is measured in units called volts. The volt is named after Volta.

Voltaic Pile Layers

copper

cloth soaked in salt water

zinc

Electrons, Right This Way!
Zinc is a conductor, or a material that allows electrons to move easily. Conductors like zinc and copper are useful for making things like electrical wires.

Series Circuit
In a series circuit, all the parts are connected in a single path.

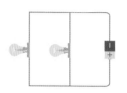

Parallel Circuit
In a parallel circuit, the current takes multiple paths to complete the circuit. If one light bulb stops working, the current will continue to flow because it still has a complete path.

In Other Words
A broken circuit is also called an open circuit. A complete circuit is also called a closed circuit.

Now that scientists could store power in batteries, they could study how electricity moves in a steady current. They learned that current only flows in a complete path, or circuit. A basic circuit includes a power source, such as a battery; a device, like a light, that will use the power; and a conductor, such as copper wires, to connect all of the parts. If any of the parts are disconnected, the circuit is broken and the current stops.

By the 1800s, scientists working on large batteries noticed something unusual. An electric current would sometimes find its own complete path and jump, or arc, between the batteries' discs. The electric arc glowed brightly.

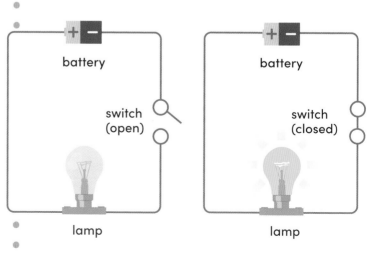

battery

switch (open)

lamp

battery

switch (closed)

lamp

Humphry Davy demonstrating his electric light

Converting Energy
Within a circuit, electrical energy can be converted into a more useful form, such as light, heat, or sound. A fan, for example, converts electricity into motion.

British scientist Humphry Davy cleverly applied this observation to invent the first electric light. He connected two wires to a battery and added charcoal strips to the end of each wire. The strips were positioned so that electricity would arc between them. His lamps produced glaring light and were used to make streetlights.

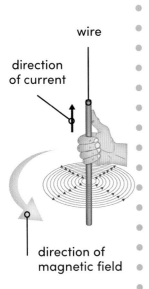

wire

direction
of current

direction of
magnetic field

Right-Hand Rule
The "right-hand
rule" can show
you the direction
of a magnetic
force around a
wire. Point your
thumb in the
direction of the
current, and curl
your fingers
around the wire.
Your fingers
show the
direction of the
magnetic force.

MYSTERIOUSLY MOVING MAGNETS

By 1820, experiments with electricity really got moving. One day, Danish scientist Hans Christian Oersted was setting up supplies for a class he was about to teach. He had one of Volta's batteries, a wire, and a magnetic compass. Oersted made a strange observation. Every time he connected the wire to the battery, the compass needle moved.

Oersted was the first to prove a connection between electricity and magnetism.

Some scientists had already noticed a connection between magnetism and electricity, but no one understood it. There are similarities between the two. Both electric charges and magnets can make things move.

Just like objects can be positively or negatively charged, the two ends, or poles, of a magnet have a positive or negative magnetic force. Opposite poles attract, or pull together. Like poles repel, or push apart. Magnets also don't have to be touching for the force between them to have an effect. They interact through an area of force around each magnet called a magnetic field.

Oersted thought about his observation for three months. He knew it was important, so he kept doing experiments. He didn't stop until he proved his theory: that an electric current in a wire produces a magnetic field.

Ampère
French physicist André-Marie Ampère built on Oersted's work. Among his accomplishments, he showed that the magnetic force around the wire is circular.

Amps
Electric current is measured in units called amps, which are named after Ampère.

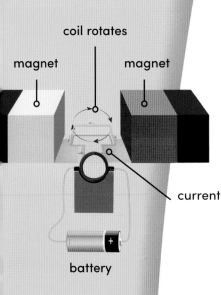

coil rotates

magnet | magnet

current

battery

Simple Motor

A basic motor consists of a wire that carries current, positioned between two magnets. The magnetic fields of the wire and the magnets interact, causing the wire to turn.

Reverse Motor

A motor can be used in reverse as a generator. If you have a small motor from a toy, you can wind it to make your own electricity.

In 1821, British scientist Michael Faraday made a simple device that could transform electricity into motion. He called it an electric magnetic rotation apparatus. Today, we call it a motor.

Michael Faraday

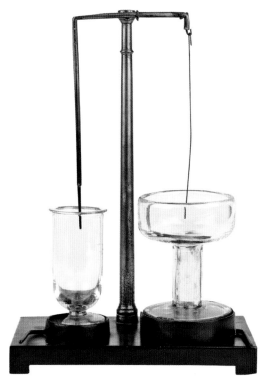

Faraday's electric motor

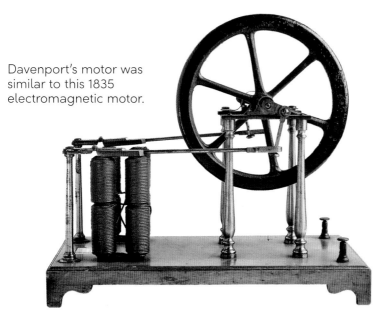
Davenport's motor was similar to this 1835 electromagnetic motor.

American inventor Thomas Davenport designed a better motor. He developed the first battery-powered motor that was powerful enough to do useful work. It supplied power to a small printing press. Davenport and his wife, Emily, also created the first electric car.

Fifty years later, engineers developed motors that could be mass produced and used in any type of machine. Today, motors are found in everything from cars to boats to refrigerators and other devices in the home. Even phones have motors in them. Every time a phone vibrates, tiny motors are at work!

The Davenports
Davenport was a blacksmith by trade. He had no formal education, just a curious mind. His wife, Emily, worked as his partner. She took detailed notes. She also gave him ideas about how to test his inventions and make them work even better.

Changing Energy
Power plants don't actually "create" energy. They simply change energy from one form to another. Turbines help transform chemical energy, nuclear energy, or another form of energy into the energy of motion. From there, generators like Faraday's transform the energy into electricity.

Special Magnets
Electromagnets can be very powerful. Unlike regular magnets, they can be turned on and off.

In 1831, Faraday made another monumental discovery. Oersted had shown that an electric current produces a magnetic field. Faraday showed that the opposite was also true: moving magnetic fields produce electric currents. With an invention called the generator, Faraday "made" electricity by rotating a metal disc in a magnetic field.

Today, power plants use that same concept to provide electricity to homes and schools. Most power plants contain machines called turbines.

Nuclear Power Plant

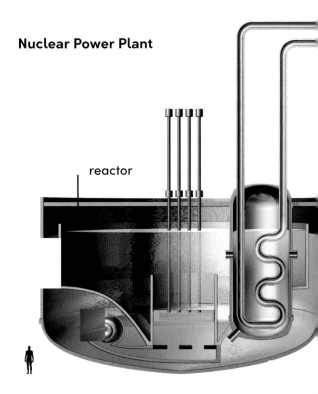

reactor

A turbine has blades like a fan. Coal, oil, natural gas, or a powerful nuclear reaction can be used to create steam. The steam is passed through the turbine's blades to make them turn.

As a turbine's blades spin, they rotate a large electromagnet inside a generator. An electromagnet is a magnet made by passing current through a wire coiled around a metal core. When it rotates, it produces electricity.

Move It!
Another term for the energy of motion is kinetic energy.

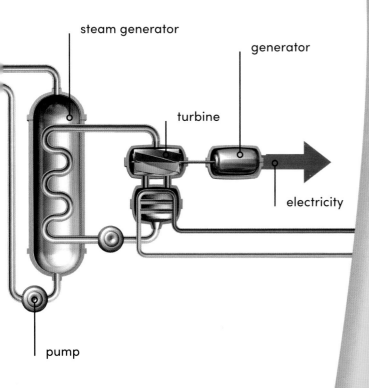

steam generator

generator

turbine

electricity

pump

Make an Electromagnet
You can make a simple electromagnet. All you need is a battery, a long iron bolt, and insulated copper wire to wrap around it. The wire can get hot, so wear gloves.

Notable Inventor
Lewis Latimer's parents were enslaved before he was born. He served in the military during the Civil War. He had no formal training in science. Yet, he became an important inventor.

LEDs
Light-emitting diode (LED) bulbs were invented in 1962. They last up to 25 times longer and use 75 percent less electricity than incandescent bulbs do.

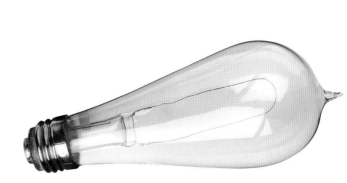

LIGHTEN UP!

By the late 1800s, city streets around the world glowed with electric arc lamps. But the lamps were expensive, unreliable, and extremely dangerous. Sparks would often fly out and start fires. Inventors strove to find a more practical solution. They needed a light bulb that people could use safely in ordinary homes.

In 1879, American inventor Thomas Edison created the first practical light bulb. It contained a filament, which is a thin fiber that glows when heated by electricity. Many other scientists soon worked to improve on the light bulb. The problem was that the filament would burn out and was expensive to make.

American inventor Lewis Latimer came up with a better filament. Latimer's carbon-filament light bulbs lasted longer than the others. In 1884, Latimer went to work with Edison at the Edison Electric Light Company. Edison and his team found ways to make the carbon-filament light bulb work even better. They created the modern version of the incandescent light bulb.

Making Light
Before electricity was available, people burned all sorts of things to light their lamps. Popular options included whale oil, kerosene, and even lard.

Thomas Edison with his incandescent lamp

Direct Current (DC)

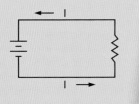

Alternating Current (AC)

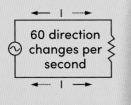

60 direction changes per second

The War of the Currents
Edison and Tesla fought hard and dirty to promote their views about electric current. Edison claimed AC current was dangerous and could kill people. Tesla shocked himself with 250,000 volts of AC power to prove it wasn't.

Edison dreamed of a day when every home would be filled with lights shining brightly—all thanks to his light bulbs. To get that dream off the ground, his company built a power station in downtown New York City in the United States.

Unfortunately, the electric current could only power a square mile around the station. The electrical energy was escaping from the wires as heat. The plant had no good way to get the electricity to homes farther away.

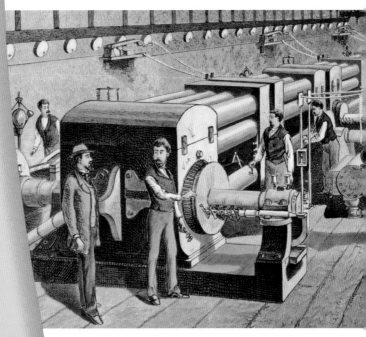

inside Edison's electric power plant

In search of a solution, Edison hired Serbian American engineer Nikola Tesla. According to some stories, Edison may have offered Tesla $50,000 (about 41,000 pounds) to improve his power system. That's about a million dollars (820,000 pounds) in today's money.

Edison's system used DC, or direct current. Direct current is current that flows in one direction. Tesla proposed using another form of current called AC, or alternating current. Alternating current switches directions many times each second. Alternating current was a good solution because it could be sent long distances over wires without losing much energy.

Legend has it that Edison never paid Tesla for solving the power problem. He may have been joking when he offered the money. No one knows for sure. Angered, Tesla left to start his own company. It turns out he was right about alternating current. Even Edison began using it, and it is still used today.

Honoring Tesla
The strength of a magnetic field is measured in units called teslas, which are named after Tesla.

A Bright Idea
Tesla's AC system was used to light up the Chicago World's Fair in 1893.

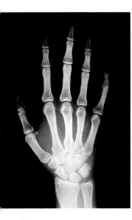

X-rays
Doctors now routinely use X–rays to see inside bodies.

Remote Controls
If you have ever used a remote control, you can thank Tesla for that, too. He invented the first remote control. He used a toy boat to demonstrate how it worked.

Now on his own, Tesla cranked out one invention after another. If you have ever had an X-ray, you can thank Tesla. His work on "shadowgraphs" led to the later invention of X-ray machines. X-rays are a form of electromagnetic radiation.

Tesla also invented the Tesla coil, a device that produces high-voltage, low-current AC electricity that turns on and off quickly. Tesla is shown demonstrating his invention in the image above. Tesla coils were used in the first wireless radios and televisions.

Eureka!
With his giant Tesla coil, Tesla created the first human-made lightning.

In 1900, Tesla designed a wireless world broadcasting tower. He hoped to provide the world with a way to share information such as weather updates and messages. Tesla didn't have enough money to finish his tower. But his prediction of a world of information sharing came true, as did the world of wireless technology.

Neon Lights
Tesla also made neon-like lights that could be used to form shapes and words. Modern neon lights are commonly used in signs.

Transformers
Transformers are devices that change the voltage of AC power. High-voltage is best for sending electric power over long distances. The voltage is lowered to safer levels before it reaches people's homes.

Historic power plant at Niagara Falls

Tesla also helped design the world's first hydroelectric power plant, which was in New York, USA. Hydroelectric plants use the force of falling water instead of steam to generate power. Tesla's power plant captured energy from the mighty Niagara Falls on the border of New York state and Ontario, Canada. As water flowed past the turbine's blades, they began to spin. This caused the generator to spin as well, producing electricity. Today's hydroelectric power plants work in much the same way.

Of course, Tesla's power system used alternating current. It also had transformers, which use huge magnets to increase or decrease the voltage of the alternating current. Transformers allow electricity to travel long distances without losing much energy. The Niagara Falls plant sent electric current all the way to the city of Buffalo, New York, which was 22 miles (35 km) away. That was quite a feat at the time.

Lifelong Dream
Tesla saw an engraving of Niagara Falls when he was a child. He imagined how he could use the water to turn a big wheel. He even told his uncle that someday he would go to America to build it.

Niagara Power
Today, the United States and Canada both have hydroelectric power plants in Niagara Falls. The plants supply about one-fourth of all the power used in New York and Ontario.

CREATING ELECTRICITY TODAY

Where does your electricity come from today? In many parts of the world, fossil fuels are used to fire up power plants. Fossil fuels include coal, natural gas, and oil. They are the remains of organisms that died long ago and were buried and compressed over time. Fossil fuels are inexpensive to use and relatively easy to store and transport. They also burn easily.

Some power plants use nuclear power to create electricity. The plants split apart atoms of uranium to create smaller atoms. This process, called nuclear fission, creates powerful nuclear reactions that produce a great amount of energy at a relatively low cost.

Coal, oil, natural gas, and uranium are all nonrenewable resources. This means they will run out. Fossil fuels do build back eventually, but the process takes millions of years. That is too long to wait!

Relying on Nonrenewables
Nonrenewable resources are used to create nearly 72 percent of the electricity people around the world use today. South Africa relies on fossil fuels the most, with 88 percent of its electricity coming from these sources. France relies on nuclear power the most. Sixty-nine percent of its electricity comes from nuclear energy.

What Is Coal?
Coal is a dark, solid fossil fuel that is found in deposits of sedimentary rock. More than half of its weight comes from carbon. Coal is found all over the world. The largest deposits are found in various parts of the United States.

What Is Oil?
Oil is a slippery liquid mainly composed of carbon and hydrogen. Most oil is found in reservoirs located in rocks underground. People drill wells to bring the oil to the surface.

What Is Natural Gas?
Natural gas is a fossil fuel mainly made up of the gas methane. It is colorless, odorless, and tasteless. Gas companies add a chemical that smells like rotten eggs to natural gas so people know when a pipeline is leaking.

What Is Uranium?
Uranium is a silvery-white metal found in soil, rocks, and water. Uranium is radioactive. Its atoms split apart easily. As they do, they release radiation, which is harmful to humans.

Climate Change
Higher average temperatures are just one sign that Earth's climate is changing. Other signs include more droughts, more severe storms, changes in rain and snow patterns, less snowpack, and warmer and more acidic oceans. In addition, sea ice is shrinking, glaciers are melting, permafrost is thawing, and sea levels are rising.

Another issue with nonrenewable resources is pollution. As fossil fuels burn, they release carbon dioxide, other gases, and particle pollution into the air. When sunlight reacts with these things, it creates a dark, heavy fog called smog. Smog is unhealthy for humans and animals and can kill plants.

Carbon dioxide is a natural part of the atmosphere. But too much of it in the atmosphere is a problem. Carbon dioxide is a greenhouse gas.

Greenhouse Effect

heat from the Sun

As carbon dioxide builds up, it and other greenhouse gases act like a blanket that traps heat close to Earth. This is the main reason why Earth's average surface temperature is steadily rising.

Completed nuclear reactions create leftover material called nuclear waste. That's another problem. Nuclear waste is hazardous and must be stored securely. Currently, more than 400,000 tons (363,000 t) of nuclear waste sits in storage centers around the world.

London smog

Los Angeles smog

Types of Smog
There are two types of smog. Sulfurous smog, also known as London smog, happens when fossil fuels—particularly coal—are burned. Photochemical smog, also known as Los Angeles smog, is fueled by automobile emissions.

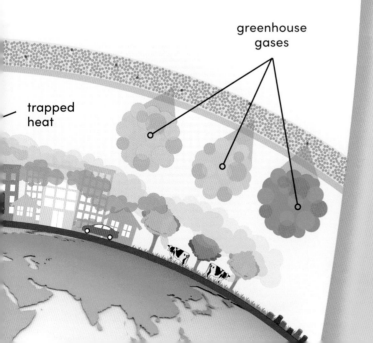

greenhouse gases

trapped heat

The Sun Queen
Hungarian American Maria Telkes was one of the founders of solar energy. She created the first solar-powered home heating system in the 1940s. Telkes earned the nickname "Sun Queen."

Concentrated solar power plants use mirrors to direct sunlight toward a central point. They offer a sustainable way to make steam to run turbines.

Fortunately, there are many renewable resources available to create electricity. These are clean sources of energy that do not pollute the environment. And they will never run out.

Geothermal energy, which is heat that comes from below Earth's surface, is one option. Geothermal energy is available all over Earth. It occurs when certain chemical elements inside Earth break down and give off heat. It is abundant near volcanoes. There, the heat is close to the surface, so it is easy to capture and use to create electricity.

Wind is another option. As the wind blows, the giant blades on wind turbines spin, creating huge amounts of electricity. The faster the wind blows, the more electricity the turbines produce.

Water can be used to create energy, too. Hydroelectric power plants capture the power of water as it flows from reservoirs. People are also working on new ways to capture the massive power of ocean waves. Special machines convert the motion and power of waves into electricity.

Wave energy will likely continue to improve, but solar power is a good option to use right now. It uses devices called solar cells to transform energy from sunlight into electricity.

A place where many wind turbines are grouped together is called a wind farm.

Ancient Energy Source
People have used wind as a source of power for a long time. For thousands of years, people built windmills to crush grain and pump water.

Electric Meters
A meter box on the outside of a home measures how much electricity people use. The electric company sends a bill for the amount used each month.

What Hours?
Electricity use is measured in watt-hours (Wh). If you use a 40-watt light bulb for one hour, you have used 40 Wh of electrical energy. The average household in the US uses nearly 30,000 Wh, or 30 kWh, of electricity each day.

BRINGING IT HOME

So, how does all of that power get from a power plant into people's homes? It travels across a grid. A grid, or power grid, is all of the pieces that make up an entire electrical system.

How does the grid work? The grid connects generators with customers, using multiple paths. For faraway customers, electricity is transformed to a higher voltage first. The high-voltage power runs through wires draped between huge steel towers.

The electricity flows through the wires. It gets closer and closer to its destination. But before it can safely enter a home, the voltage must be reduced. So, the power flows into substations where transformers reduce the voltage.

Local wires connect the electrical system to homes and businesses. There, more transformers further reduce the voltage. Finally, the electricity is flowing at the right rate to enter a home. A wire connects the grid to the outside of the home. More wires, running throughout the home, connect to outlets.

Now, people can plug in and use the electricity. And ever so slowly, the grid is expanding so people can easily plug in a variety of environmentally friendly products such as electric cars, e-scooters, and e-bikes. There are even charging stations to plug into when you need to charge your electric car away from home.

Plugging In
Across the world, electricity use has more than tripled in just the past 40 years.

Conserving Energy
People in the United States waste about 35 percent of the electrical energy they use. To conserve energy, use more LED light bulbs and energy-efficient appliances. Use less air-conditioning and heating. Turn off lights and devices when not using them. And don't leave the fridge door open for so long when searching for a snack.

Transforming Lives

Having access to electricity allows businesses, hospitals, and schools to use newer technologies. It lets students study into the night. Electricity also makes communities safer. People no longer have to burn dangerous straw fires in their homes to see on pitch-black nights.

Despite all the electricity used globally, there are millions of people who don't have access to electricity. They may live far from the nearest electrical grid. Many people who can't just flick a switch to turn on the lights use kerosene oil to light lamps instead. But burning kerosene can be harmful to people's health.

Burning kerosene indoors can cause fires and explosions. Breathing in its fumes for long periods of time may also lead to lung diseases and cancer.

A British organization called SolarAid set out to solve this problem. They wanted to help people living in southern Africa who didn't have electricity. The organization asked two inventors, Martin Riddiford and Jim Reeves, for help.

Riddiford and Reeves created a device that got the energy it needed from two simple and free sources—human power and gravity. To turn the light on, the user lifted a weight. As the weight slowly fell back down, it rotated a generator that powered the light. But the light wasn't bright enough and it didn't shine long enough.

The inventors made a brighter light. Then, they created an even better product. The user simply pulls on a cord for one minute and a bright light shines for up to two hours. Users can also plug into USB ports to charge mobile devices.

Wind Power
There are several ways to make your own electricity. Vertical wind turbines are quiet and harmless to wildlife. You can even buy them for your home.

Wearable Electricity
New wearable solar cells are being designed for people to make electricity on the go.

Huygens probe

Batteries in Space
Some space missions are short. Batteries supply all the energy the spacecraft need. The Huygens probe was only expected to work for a few hours as it fell toward the surface of Titan, Saturn's largest moon.

Living far from a power grid is one thing. But what about the people and spacecraft that explore outer space? Where do they get the electricity they need to keep going once they leave Earth?

Some spacecraft, like the Mars Reconnaissance Orbiter, rely on the Sun. During the day, solar panels capture the Sun's energy and convert it into electricity. Some of that energy is stored in rechargeable batteries that keep the satellite moving at night.

Hydrogen gas gives rockets the power they need to blast off Earth's surface. Hydrogen fuel cells supply energy to a spacecraft's electrical systems. Fuel cells convert hydrogen and oxygen into water. During that process, they produce electricity and heat.

Fuel cells do require a source of hydrogen. But they operate like a battery that never runs down and never needs to be recharged. Because of that, they are an important factor as people set out to go to the planet Mars. Fuel cells could provide the electricity people need to survive there.

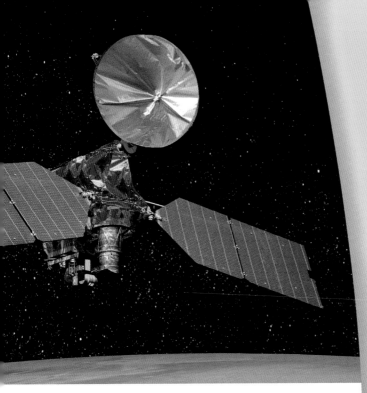

Mars Reconnaissance Orbiter

In the future, people will need new ways to make electricity on Earth and beyond. New inventions make this possible. What will the future of electricity look like? Maybe YOU will be one of the next inventors who decides.

Getting Energy from Atoms
Everything is made of atoms, the tiny building blocks of matter. Some atoms, called radioisotopes, are unstable and fall apart. As they do, they release energy as heat. That is how the Perseverance rover creates electricity as it explores Mars. The rover uses heat produced when plutonium decays to make electricity.

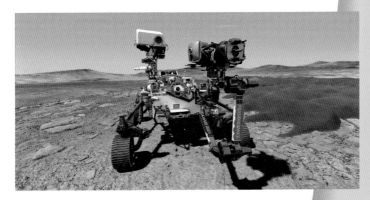

Perseverance rover on Mars

GLOSSARY

Alternating current (AC)
Electric current that regularly
switches direction as it flows

Battery
A device that stores energy to use
as a source of electricity

Circuit
The complete path of an
electric current

Conductor
A material that allows electricity
to flow through it

Direct current (DC)
Electric current that only flows in
one direction

Electricity
A type of energy resulting from
charged particles

Electron
A particle of an atom with a
negative charge

Electric charge
An imbalance of protons
and electrons

Electric current
The movement of electrons

Filament
A thread that produces light when
current passes through it

Fossil fuel
Fuel made of the remains of plants
and animals that lived millions of
years ago

Generator
A device that transforms kinetic
energy into electrical energy

Geothermal
Energy inside Earth

Hydroelectric
Energy from moving water

Kinetic energy
The energy of motion

Magnetic field
The area of force surrounding
a magnet

Motor
A device that transforms electrical
energy into kinetic energy

Power plant
A place where electricity is
generated from another source
of energy

Proton
A particle of an atom with a
positive charge

Solar cell
A device that transforms energy
from sunlight into electricity

Static electricity
The movement of electrons from
one material to another

Turbine
A device that rotates to turn a
generator and produce electricity

INDEX

QUIZ

Answer the questions to see what you have learned. Check your answers in the key below.

1. What type of electricity made Benjamin Franklin's trick spiders move?

2. What did Alessandro Volta invent to store electrical energy?

3. What is a circuit?

4. What did Hans Christian Oersted discover?

5. True or False: A motor transforms electricity into kinetic energy.

6. Which type of current did Nikola Tesla generate?

7. What type of renewable energy comes from deep within Earth?

8. What is the electricity system that brings power to your home called?

1. Static electricity 2. The battery 3. The complete path of an electric current 4. An electric current in a wire produces a magnetic field 5. True 6. Alternating current (AC) 7. Geothermal 8. A grid